Ask Her

JANE TRUFANT HARVEY

Simple Words to Jumpstart Your Conversation with Mary

Published by Wellspring
An Imprint of Viident

The quotes in this book have been drawn from dozens of sources. They are assumed to be accurate as quoted in their previously published forms. Although every effort has been made to verify the quotes and sources, the Publisher cannot guarantee their perfect accuracy.

Designed by Ashley Dias

ISBN: 978-1-63582-230-4 (hardcover)
ISBN: 978-1-63582-231-1 (eBook)

10 9 8 7 6 5 4 3 2 1

Printed in the United States of America

Author's Note

The first thing I did when Matthew Kelly asked me to write this book was to prayerfully ask Mary to reveal herself to me. What was her heart really like? How did she love? What did she want me to learn?

And so it began, these beautiful and profound exchanges she and I had in prayer. I read about her. I studied her. I asked if she would inspire in me the things that were important to *her.*

She became alive for me. I discovered a soul full of love. I discovered her mother's heart, her gentle spirit, her incalculable desire for us to know her Son, her passion to teach us how to grow in holiness. Her unrelenting endeavor to do whatever she can to guide us to heaven.

She taught me about faith and being faithful. She taught me

about courage and obedience, about trust, about being trustworthy. She taught me about the incredible beauty of humility.

She is without question love personified, just like her Son.

This book certainly didn't happen all at once. She took time with me. She taught me, instructed me, loved me. She was gentle, but forthright, and so patient.

I feel such enormous gratitude to her and for her.

My sincerest prayer is that I was able to take everything I have learned, discovered, and encountered and convey it in such a way that you would be able to know and experience the very essence of Mary, the extraordinary Mother of our Savior.

I wrote 365 "Ask Her" prayer prompts for you. One for each day. My prayer is that you will not just have an experience with Our Lady, but that you will have an *encounter* with her. An experience is a meeting or a moment when something happens, but an encounter is when something unexpectedly *new* happens. I want that for you!

I am forever changed because I wrote this book and I pray with all my heart that when you read it, you will be too!

Momma Mary, thank you for always loving us and pointing us to your Son!

Pray for us, oh Holy Mother of God, that we may be made worthy of the promises of Christ.

JANE TRUFANT HARVEY

Ask Her

1.

Ask Her...

to remind you that you will not
crumble under the weight of fear.
You will rise up and overcome!
You will conquer through GRACE!
Because THAT is the will of God for you!

2.

Ask Her...

to challenge you to purposefully find
something to be grateful for every day.

3.

Ask Her...

to remind you that her Son did not judge. Instead, He welcomed the most deplorable of sinners under His roof. You are called to do the same, to exemplify that compassionate love.

4.

Ask Her...

to inspire you to believe in the best of someone when no one else will.

5.

Ask Her...

to remind you that life is fleeting. Choose joy!

6.

Ask Her...

to help you remember that, from the very beginning, her Son relied on others to spread His Gospel messages. Today, He's relying on you!

7.

Ask Her...

to remind you of how strong and resilient you are, and that she will ALWAYS be your advocate.

8.

Ask Her...

to let her unimaginable love for you permeate any empty spaces in your heart.

9.

Ask Her...

to remind you that helping others is good for the soul.

10.

Ask Her...

to remind you that God did not make you to "fit in," He made you to stand out!

11.

Ask Her...

to remind you of the remarkable reality that God's grace, indwelling power, and presence are at work within you!

12.

Ask Her...

to remind you, if someone you love suffers from addiction, she's right beside you, praying for their deliverance and peace.

13.

Ask Her...

to help you remember that extreme hurt often requires extreme forgiveness.

14.

Ask Her...

to remind you that one of the most incredible things you can do for yourself is to partner with God with the intentional purpose of self-transformation.

15.

Ask Her...

to help you recognize how much time you might be spending trying to control the perceptions other people have of you.

16.

Ask Her...

to remind you that you don't have to apologize for what you have. When you are grateful for what you have, you honor the generosity of her Son.

17.

Ask Her...

to teach you that when you stumble, you should fall into the mercy of her Son, not away from it.

18.

Ask Her...

to help you prayerfully examine whether you would be able to live up to the high standards you set for others.

19.

Ask Her...

to remind you, when the people you love are struggling and you can't do anything to fix it, that just being present with them does more than you could imagine.

20.

Ask Her…

to help you grasp the magnitude of her Son's baptism. Jesus placed the very worst of humanity, the burden and guilt of all mankind, on His shoulders and carried it into the depths of the Jordan River.

21.

Ask Her…

to help you be an example of the virtues you hope your children and grandchildren will emulate.

22.
Ask Her...

if today you would recognize an opportunity to do a random act of kindness for someone. It's in the smallest acts of caring that we change the lives of others.

23.
Ask Her...

if she'd help you truly embrace that it's okay to be broken, afraid, or weak. You might make mistakes, cause calamity, or have lapses in judgment. But no matter what, you will always be intrinsically worthy of love.

24.

Ask Her...

if she would help instill in you
a deep and profound acceptance
of all that makes you, you!

25.

Ask Her...

to remind you that apologizing to
your children when you've made
a mistake is life-changing for *them*.

26.

Ask Her...

to give you the grace and fortitude
to forgive someone who isn't sorry.

27.

Ask Her...

to remind you that she watched
her Son suffer and die. If you are facing
the death of someone you love, she
understands your anguish and will be
there to strengthen and sustain you.

28.

Ask Her…

to help you remember that *your* attitude can be such a compelling example to others that it can completely change the trajectory of *their* lives.

29.

Ask Her…

to remind you that God has plans for you: "Plans to prosper you, not to harm you, to give you hope and a future." Don't let anyone ever tell you differently!

30.

Ask Her...

on the days you're feeling unsure
of yourself, if she'd help you embrace
this truth: You are worthy of love and
affection...you're never too much...
you're always enough...you are
cherished and loved above all things
by the Creator of all things.

31.

Ask Her...

if she'd help you see how life's challenges stretch you, teach you, and push you to be a better version of yourself.

32.

Ask Her...

to guide you to pray with your heart, so that your prayers become an effortless and beautiful exchange between you and God.

33.

Ask Her...

to help you believe that your life can be transfigured by the brilliant light emanating from the Heart of Christ.

34.

Ask Her...

if she'd help you remember how important and affirming it is when you put yourself in someone else's shoes and validate their feelings.

35.

Ask Her...

to remind you that she wants
to bring you closer to
the heart of her Son, Jesus.

36.

Ask Her...

to remind you that just as she
delivered Christ over 2,000 years ago,
we too are called to "deliver"
Christ into our own families, our
communities, and into the world.

37.

Ask Her...

to remind you that she intercedes for you before the throne of God every day!

38.

Ask Her...

to help you remember that constant prayer is to be in constant union with the grace of God.

39.

Ask Her...

to remind you that she is here
to help lead you to Heaven.

40.

Ask Her...

if she'd help you remember that
when you place God first, your life
becomes a reflection of Him.

41.

Ask Her...

to reassure you that the best way
to approach anything is with great joy
and humility.

42.

Ask Her...

to unite with you in prayer
for the salvation of the world.

43.

Ask Her...

to remind you that her Son wants
you to cast all your cares on Him:
your distress, your anxiety, your fears,
and anything else burdening you.
Releasing these things to Him allows
Him to release his peace in you.

44.

Ask Her...

to help you discover the peace
that follows when you're
able to completely surrender
and accept God's will.

45.

Ask Her...

if she'd encourage you to reach
out to someone who is struggling
and ask how you can help.

46.

Ask Her...

to remind you that whoever acts in the light of merciful love and truth is always helped by Heaven.

47.

Ask Her...

to help you understand that when you're overwhelmed and anxious, she wants to help. Go grab your rosary!

48.

Ask Her...

to help you shower love and appreciation on those who have been given the responsibility to lead and guide you in your faith.

49.

Ask Her...

to remind you that your life is not measured by the words you speak, but rather by the deeds that glorify God.

50.

Ask Her...

to help you recognize how easily you get lost in material and human things.

51.

Ask Her...

to teach you how to confidently trust that when *you* feel totally out of control, *God's* totally in control.

52.

Ask Her...

to keep you on the path to salvation.

53.

Ask Her...

to release her unshakable
peace in you and protect you from
all that chaos seeks to destroy.

54.
Ask Her...

to unite your human heart with
her Immaculate Heart.

55.
Ask Her...

if she'd bless you with her maternal
patience, especially on the days
your children are making you question
if you'll survive parenthood.

56.

Ask Her...

to encourage you to not just
speak about peace, but to live it.

57.

Ask Her...

to help you have faith that, although
Satan is busy at work in this world,
she is also busy praying for the
protection over all that is holy!

58.

Ask Her...

to show you all the ways you can make your life a continuous prayer.

59.

Ask Her...

to help take away any feelings of jealousy for the things you wish you had and replace them with feelings of gratitude for the things you've been given.

60.

Ask Her...

if today, she would help you make a conscious effort to be agreeable instead of difficult.

61.

Ask Her...

to remind you that she delights in helping you live your life as a joyful testimony for Jesus.

62.

Ask Her...

to help you be an example of
how merciful love leads to healing
and restoration in a family.

63.

Ask Her...

to remind you that she prays every day
for peace in your heart, peace in your
family, and peace in your relationships.

64.

Ask Her...

to reveal how life-changing it can be to begin each morning with prayer and end each evening with thanksgiving.

65.

Ask Her...

when you're feeling unsettled, to remind you there is an order to things: First, God. Second, your spouse. Third, your children. Make sure these things are not out of order.

66.

Ask Her...

to remind you that humanity
is in desperate need of spiritual
comfort; she'd like you to be
the hands and feet of Christ
to offer that comfort.

67.

Ask Her...

to remind you that the way
to shape the souls of the next
generation is to humbly bare your
imperfections and allow yourself to
be transformed by the Holy Spirit.

68.
Ask Her...

to remind you that prayer is the foundation of peace. You cannot have real, sustained peace if your heart is not at peace with God.

69.
Ask Her...

to remind you that it's not just about "going" to Mass; it's about "living" the Mass.

70.

Ask Her...

to remind you that you cannot speak on prayer if you do not pray.

71.

Ask Her...

if she'd remind you over and over again that if you have God, you have everything.

72.
Ask Her...

to empower you to reject any negative self-talk and replace it with these affirming truths: I am loveable. My needs and wants are important. I trust myself. I can do it!

73.
Ask Her...

to remind you that, unbeknownst to you, you could be the only "church" some people will ever know.

74.

Ask Her...

to challenge you to spend as much effort as you do being financially secure into being spiritually secure.

75.

Ask Her...

to remind you that every time Satan instigates confusion and unrest, God instigates clarity and grace.

76.

Ask Her...

to rebuke the lie that God is far away.
He has never been closer to you!

77.

Ask Her...

to remind you that the one who trusts
God is not afraid of the future.

78.

Ask Her...

to remind you that you've been specifically chosen to be a witness of peace and joy! Carry on!

79.

Ask Her...

to help you understand that the less often you think of yourself, the more content you'll be.

80.

Ask Her...

to remind you that she needs you
to be the one she can count on to love
those who nobody else loves.

81.

Ask Her...

to remind you that prayer has the power
to completely disarm the evil one.

82.

Ask Her...

to invite you into reconciliation with God!

83.

Ask Her...

to reassure you that she sees how tired you are. Go rest in front of her Son in the Blessed Sacrament, where the weariest of souls are strengthened and refreshed.

84.

Ask Her...

to help you remember that God wants to co-partner with you in the unfolding of His plan for your life.

85.

Ask Her...

to remind you to pray, especially before the cross from which great graces flow.

86.

Ask Her...

to let you know she's here
for you if you need anything.

87.

Ask Her...

to clothe you in holiness, goodness,
and obedience, so that each day you
become more prepared for Heaven.

88.

Ask Her...

if she'd help you build a reputation for being reliable and dependable.

89.

Ask Her...

for integrity and truth to prevail, ALWAYS!

90.

Ask Her...

to remind you that she will not compel you to be a saint by force. Her desire is that day by day, through your own self-denials, you will be led closer to holiness.

91.

Ask Her...

to pray with you every day for the souls in purgatory.

92.

Ask Her...

to help you decide that today
is for God!

93.

Ask Her...

to remind you that her Son longs
to set you free and purify you from
all your past transgressions.

94.

Ask Her...

to remind you that NO ONE is
so lost they can't be found by God.
NO ONE!

95.

Ask Her...

to remind you of how uniquely
loved you are in Christ's eyes,
especially in moments when you
are comparing yourself to others.

96.

Ask Her...

to remind you that her desire is for the whole world to know the God of joy, and for your life to bear witness to that joy.

97.

Ask Her...

to remind you that, with faith in God, anything is possible.

98.

Ask Her...

to remind you that she is always near, tenderly watching over you.

99.

Ask Her...

to remind you that faith can't exist without prayer.

100.

Ask Her...

to remind you that the best
"soul" food is found in the scriptures,
not in a restaurant.

101.

Ask Her...

if she'd help you encourage
other people by verbally expressing
your admiration of them.

102.

Ask Her...

to remind you that the spirit of the living God wants to get to know *you* better.

103.

Ask Her...

to help you, in your most difficult times, say, "Let it be done to me, according to Your will."

104.

Ask Her...

to remind you of this simple,
yet profound, fact: Everything around you
changes when you change yourself.

105.

Ask Her...

to remind you that she and her Son
can take the broken version of you and
transform it into the best version of you.

106.
Ask Her...

to remind you that when your *life* speaks truth, instead of your mouth, people will begin to pay attention.

107.
Ask Her...

when you feel like you don't matter to anyone, if she would remind you that you've been spoken for by the Savior of the world. He has called you by name and you are His — ALWAYS.

108.

Ask Her...

to remind you that her Son will
always speak love over you,
no matter what you have done in the
past that you feel is inexcusable.

109.

Ask Her...

to let you know that she notices
you in a special way: in the warmth of
your smile, in the kindness of your heart,
and in the stillness of your spirit.

110.

Ask Her...

to remind you that she speaks to her Son about you all the time!

111.

Ask Her...

to keep you from thinking that if you just had enough money, you would be satisfied. True contentment is rooted in knowing that God is your hope and strength, and that He will meet all your needs.

112.

Ask Her...

to help you learn how to perfectly love your imperfect self!

113.

Ask Her...

to help you remember that being on time shows honor and respect for other people's time.

114.

Ask Her...

to remind you that tolerance and empathy are the catalysts for some much-needed healing in this world!

115.

Ask Her...

if she'd help you remember that doing God's work is more about relationships than religion.

116.
Ask Her...

to help you become more aware of
how often you've finished your prayers
without ever really entering into them.

117.
Ask Her...

if she will help you be the sensitivity that
this world so desperately needs.

118.

Ask Her...

to help you advocate for fairness,
even when life is not fair.

119.

Ask Her...

to remind you that your identity
is NEVER found in someone else's
definition of you.

120.
Ask Her...

to help you start the day with surrender. Gently lay down your will, your expectations, and your ego and relinquish your desire to control how the day will unfold.

121.
Ask Her...

to remind you that the wounds of abuse are never too deep that they can't be reached by God.

122.
Ask Her...

to help you love others unselfishly and without motive for personal benefit.

123.
Ask Her...

to remind you that Eucharistic adoration generates powerful, life-giving, life-changing spiritual clarity, blessings, and peace.
GO AND BE CHANGED.

124.

Ask Her...

to encourage you to give someone the benefit of the doubt, even when you don't think they deserve it.

125.

Ask Her...

to teach you how to take all your inner turmoil, disappointment, hurt, embarrassment, inadequacy, fear, anger, confusion, and heartbreak AND LEAVE IT, ALL OF IT at the foot of the cross!

126.

Ask Her...

to help you choose every day
to perpetuate good!

127.

Ask Her...

for the courage to be willing to
stand alone for what is right.

128.

Ask Her...

to help you remember not to worry when you're feeling disconnected from her Son. She'll be the bridge.

129.

Ask Her...

if she would help you, not just to pray, but to truly encounter God in prayer.

130.

Ask Her...

if today she would help you remember to smile at and verbally acknowledge every single person you encounter.

131.

Ask Her...

during the times you feel let down and discouraged, if she would carry you toward the marvelous love and consolation of her Son.

132.

Ask Her...

to help you be fearless about proclaiming and protecting the sanctity of life.

133.

Ask Her...

to help you remember that when you adore Jesus, you honor her.

134.
Ask Her...

to teach you how to offer
your suffering as a gift to God.

135.
Ask Her...

to help you see that dissatisfaction
often manifests itself when you're trying
to do things without God.

136.

Ask Her…

to teach you how to yield your heart to God, so nothing can impede the work the Holy Spirit wants to accomplish in you.

137.

Ask Her…

to remind you that prayer is the union of hearts in love and devotion.

138.

Ask Her...

if she will help you see the cross as a signpost of love and forgiveness through which peace comes.

139.

Ask Her...

to remind you that she's always excited to spend time with you!

140.
Ask Her...

to remind you that the more you covet material things, the further you are from eternal things.

141.
Ask Her...

to help you trust that there is nothing in your future that you and God can't handle together.

142.

Ask Her...

to remind you that, when you're tempted by sin, earth is only a short stop between this moment and eternity. Choose wisely!

143.

Ask Her...

if she could help you find the courage to be honest with yourself and with others.

144.

Ask Her...

to encourage you to reach out
and discover the tremendous inspiration
and power of group prayer.

145.

Ask Her...

to remind you, if you're
looking for hope, look for her Son.
They're interchangeable.

146.

Ask Her...

to remind you that if you truly want to be awed by God, simply step into the beauty and brilliance of nature.

147.

Ask Her...

if she'd help you make a humble pledge to put love above EVERYTHING ELSE.

148.

Ask Her...

if she'd help you remember that
even though there are times God feels
near and other times it's not so clear,
He NEVER leaves you.

149.

Ask Her...

to remind you that even when
rejection can feel personal, NOTHING
will ever thwart what God has already
destined for you. Trust!

150.

Ask Her...

to reaffirm that your innate value as a human being is not measured by your achievements. You have innate value simply because you exist.

151.

Ask Her...

if she'd help you see that each day you die a little more *to* self is another day you're living a little more *for* Christ.

152.

Ask Her...

to assure you that God has chosen *you* as part of His plan for the salvation of mankind. Don't underestimate the value of your role in His design.

153.

Ask Her...

to remind you that you have all the qualities to be a model of gentleness in this harsh world. Share them!

154.

Ask Her...

to surround you with people of good character for you to emulate!

155.

Ask Her...

to remind you that tears are prayer offerings to God.

156.

Ask Her...

to remind you she doesn't want you to settle for any relationship unless you're valued and cherished and treated with affection and tenderness.

157.

Ask Her...

to give you the humility to invite God into your suffering and to use it to purify you and refine His radiance in you.

158.

Ask Her...

to pray that God would come into the hardened parts of your heart and make them pliable, obedient, and ready to serve.

159.

Ask Her...

to remind you in these unprecedented times of change, God does not change. His face will shine upon you, He will give you peace, and His favor will rest upon you and your family.

160.

Ask Her...

to remind you that each time
your decisions are framed by kindness,
you cultivate new possibilities
for peace and goodwill.

161.

Ask Her...

to remind you that *you* matter.
You are not alone. You are wanted!
Loved! Necessary!

162.

Ask Her...

to remind you that you can be powerful *and* ask for help at the same time.

163.

Ask Her...

to help you understand how important it is to be a person who honors their word and who is trusted to keep a confidence.

164.
Ask Her...

to help you resist the temptation
to slightly alter the truth. Remember,
your word is your bond.

165.
Ask Her...

to help you remember that
her Son is your place of safety,
a refuge for you. Go to Him,
even if it's only for a minute.

166.

Ask Her...

to instill in you the healing gift of listening compassionately to the sorrow, pain, and suffering of others.

167.

Ask Her...

to give you the courage to allow others to help you, to let them take care of you, to admit that you need them.

168.

Ask Her...

to remind you that when you have a heavy cross to bear, don't be afraid to carry it. She and her Son are there to help you.

169.

Ask Her...

to remind you that repenting requires a change in behavior, not just sorrow in the heart.

170.

Ask Her...

to encourage you to not have an agenda today. Give your mind, your heart, and your weary soul a rest from the pressure to be productive. Just be.

171.

Ask Her...

to teach you that taking a leap of faith is oftentimes seen as reckless. But for the faithful, it's about trusting beyond the edges of human understanding that God is in control and wants the very best for us.

172.

Ask Her...

to keep you from being deceived into thinking that the busier you are for Jesus is what gives your faith journey meaning and purpose. Be still and listen.

173.

Ask Her...

if she'd help you channel any stubbornness into a relentless fight for truth and justice.

174.

Ask Her...

to remind you of the great graces that emerge when you pray in the presence of Christ in the Eucharist.

175.

Ask Her...

to remind you that surrender is synonymous with tranquility, which is synonymous with peace, which is synonymous with Jesus.

176.

Ask Her...

to keep reminding you of all the people desperately hurting today who might need your smile.

177.

Ask Her...

for a gentle nudge when you're being grumpy or disagreeable.

178.

Ask Her...

to reassure you that you are not the only one who may struggle to understand the Bible. Remember, you don't have to understand *everything* to learn *something*!

179.

Ask Her...

to help you discern which people in your life are helping or hindering you in becoming the best version of yourself.

180.
Ask Her...

to encourage you to be like Jesus — take time to withdraw from your busy life to pray and focus your attention on what's most important.

181.
Ask Her...

to make you aware that there is no such thing as a "chance" encounter. Every interaction you have is purposed by God for you to either learn something, teach something, or both!

182.

Ask Her...

to remind you that honesty, integrity, and truth are virtues that earn respect in both the eyes of the world and the eyes of God.

183.

Ask Her...

to help you stand firm when you say you trust God's plan, so you won't be tempted to change course if you don't think He's acting fast enough.

184.

Ask Her...

to remind you that, from her own personal experience, A LOT can happen in three days!

185.

Ask Her...

to help you contemplate the amazing change we'd have in the world if we started "catching" people doing something good instead of when they falter.

186.

Ask Her...

to reveal how an act of obedience to God is worthy. But when the act is prefaced with a spirit of obedience, it is praiseworthy.

187.

Ask Her...

to protect your heart from allowing the toxicity of negative people to seep into the beauty of who you are.

188.

Ask Her...

to help you remember that when you speak healing words to a wounded soul, you are reflecting exactly what Jesus came to this earth to do.

189.

Ask Her...

to help you consider that, although it's part of the human condition to want to take the path of least resistance, the easiest way is not often the right way.

190.

Ask Her…

if she'd show you how to summon the strength and humility to choose the high road, especially if you're feeling angry or vindictive.

191.

Ask Her…

to help your prayer and surrender to God become road signs, guiding others toward Him.

192.
Ask Her...

to make you aware of how frequently disillusionment in relationships is related to unmet expectations that simply haven't been communicated.

193.
Ask Her...

to remind you that the beauty of fasting is in your willingness to say no to yourself and yes to God. It's these acts of self-discipline and self-restraint that strip the body and exalt the soul.

194.

Ask Her...

to remind you, with God, you can be vulnerable with the most fragile parts of yourself.

195.

Ask Her...

to help you remember that there's renewal and restoration in reconciliation.

196.

Ask Her...

to help you discern if there is someone in your life you might need to be a little nicer to!

197.

Ask Her...

to reassure you that there is NOT. ONE. THING. WHAT. SO. EVER that can interfere with God's ultimate vision for you.

198.

Ask Her...

to help you more confidently
trust that when you have problems,
God has solutions!

199.

Ask Her...

when you're worrying about the future,
to remind you that God goes before you,
setting things in motion, and making sure
everything falls into its proper place.

200.

Ask Her...

to help you remember that God does not waste ANYTHING. What you're enduring now will be used to accomplish transforming goodness, in both yourself and the world, according to His plan.

201.

Ask Her...

to remind you that every person you see today is wrestling with personal burdens that can't be seen from the outside.

202.

Ask Her...

to remind you that, just as she stood and wept at the foot of her Son's cross, she will stand and weep with you at the foot of yours.

203.

Ask Her...

to remind you when someone you love makes a life-altering mistake, what they need most is your unconditional love and mercy.

204.

Ask Her...

to remind you that goodness, gentleness, wisdom, understanding, fortitude, reverence, love, joy, peace, patience, kindness, and faithfulness are not man-made virtues. They are God-made.

205.

Ask Her...

if she'd help you remember that your value doesn't come from who you are, but whose you are!

206.
Ask Her...

if she'd help you extend a heart of mercy when you're frustrated, rather than one of chastisement and retribution.

207.
Ask Her...

to help you grasp how truly extraordinary God's design is that your humanity would be interwoven with His divinity.

208.

Ask Her...

if she'd help you sort out the things
you may focus too much attention
on that don't really matter.

209.

Ask Her...

to bless you with her strength
and fortitude so you too will have
the courage to say "yes" to God in the
face of unimaginable circumstances.

210.

Ask Her...

to help you truly grasp that you exist today because, in God's ultimate plan for the world, He needed *you* to be here right now, at this EXACT moment in time. Let the magnitude of that sink in...

211.

Ask Her...

if she'd pray that kindheartedness sets the tone for your whole household.

212.
Ask Her...

to remind you that great healing can come by doing absolutely nothing except sitting quietly in God's holy presence.

213.
Ask Her...

to teach you that praising God in the storm helps shift the focus from your circumstances to trusting that someone more powerful is in charge.

214.

Ask Her...

to remind you that you don't have to preach the message to lead others to God. Live the message.

215.

Ask Her...

to remind you that sometimes you won't be able to see that God is all you need...until God is all you have.

216.

Ask Her...

to help you trust that her Son
will complete you like no other person
or possession ever could.

217.

Ask Her...

to show you how recognizing
your own shortcomings can
make you more compassionate
to the shortcomings of others.

218.
Ask Her...

to assure you of her great empathy
during those times you aren't able
to take away the pain or heartache
your children encounter.

219.
Ask Her...

to help you realize how holding
on to anger and resentment is like
locking yourself in an emotional
prison and giving away the key
to peace and healing.

220.

Ask Her...

to give you the grace to stand up to protect someone's dignity, even if you don't agree with their lifestyle.

221.

Ask Her...

to remind you that, in a sincere and profound way, she knows the unbearable pain of losing a child. As your Heavenly Mother, she prays unceasingly for divine consolation to comfort any parent who lives with this anguish.

222.

Ask Her...

to help you remember that
YOU are a beloved child of God
and on you, His favor rests.

223.

Ask Her...

if she would teach you that "to fear
the Lord" doesn't mean to be
afraid of Him. It means to love Him,
to be in reverent awe of His holiness,
and to honor and respect Him.

224.

Ask Her...

to teach you how to step outside
of yourself and into the needs of others.

225.

Ask Her...

to remind you that one of the most
beautiful things you can do is to affirm
the goodness in others.

226.
Ask Her…

to help encourage your family to list the things that make them grateful, then pray for the people in the world who might not have those things.

227.
Ask Her…

to help you learn to be intentional… intentional in worship, intentional in prayer, intentional in humility, intentional in love, and intentional in_______________. (You fill in the blank).

228.

Ask Her...

if she'd remind you that it doesn't matter if you've known God all your life or if you only turned to God now. He doesn't care why or how you found Him, only that you did. He's been waiting for you.

229.

Ask Her...

if she'd remind you that even though it's not guaranteed you'll see the harvest, don't ever stop sowing the seeds.

230.

Ask Her...

if she'll help you realize that if it's not challenging you, it's not changing you.

231.

Ask Her...

to make sure you're very clear that failure is an event, not a person.

232.
Ask Her...

to remind you it's okay to be disappointed with yourself, or someone else, or even with God. Your disappointment is not your destination.

233.
Ask Her...

if she'd help you find ways to lend your support to someone who's emotionally or physically exhausted.

234.

Ask Her...

in the moments you feel most compelled to give up, to remind you, you can do all things through Christ who strengthens you.

235.

Ask Her...

to make sure you know that every day, she is praying for you, for those you love, and for all that brings you feelings of warmth and well-being.

236.

Ask Her...

if she'll help you stay humble in your triumphs and remember that when much is given, much is expected.

237.

Ask Her...

to take away your need to be right and replace it with a heart that welcomes compromise and respects the opinions of others.

238.
Ask Her...

if she would protect your
light from being diminished by
the critical voices of others.

239.
Ask Her...

to help you try to remember that
hurt and anger are only magnified
when you hold onto them.

240.
Ask Her...

if she'd tell her Son how grateful you are for His sacrifice and the privilege of receiving Him — body, blood, soul, and divinity — in the Eucharist.

241.
Ask Her...

to really encourage *you* to be the one who reaches out to start the process of restoring any broken relationships in your life.

242.

Ask Her...

to help you exist for the praise of God's glory!

243.

Ask Her...

when you are blessed with moments of silence, to help you resist the temptation to fill them with noise.

244.

Ask Her...

if she would remind you how necessary and healing it is to give yourself time for rest and renewal.

245.

Ask Her...

to remind you that Jesus used the cooperation of the boy to multiply the loaves and fish. Be the boy!

246.
Ask Her...

if today she would help you have more faith in God's timing.

247.
Ask Her...

to remind you that if you fall, her Son will raise you. If you fall again, and again, and again...her Son will raise you.

248.

Ask Her...

to remind you to never underestimate the power of prayer and fasting.

249.

Ask Her...

if she'd teach you to entrust yourself more fully to the Holy Spirit.

250.
Ask Her...

to help you identify exactly what it is that's keeping you from crossing that river into the Promised Land.

251.
Ask Her...

to help you remember to let God's forgiveness be enough, because it IS enough!

252.

Ask Her...

if she'd help you conquer any fear that is preventing you from reaching your God-given potential.

253.

Ask Her...

to help you remember that words have the capacity to either encourage or cause damage. Choose them carefully.

254.

Ask Her...

if she'd remind you how extraordinary it is when you are a voice of encouragement to someone who's going through a rough time.

255.

Ask Her...

to remind you that it's simple: if you want to discover the meaning of life, discover the word of God.

256.

Ask Her...

to remind you that well done
is better than well said.

257.

Ask Her...

to open your eyes to the realization
that you are part of a giant tapestry
that God is weaving. Be patient.
Every thread has its unique place, in its
unique time, and with divine purpose.

258.

Ask Her...

to remind you that she doesn't want you to just stop and smell the roses, she wants you to lead others to the garden.

259.

Ask Her...

to help you focus more on what God wants FOR you instead of what God wants FROM you.

260.
Ask Her…

if she'd help you create an
environment of love and shelter
for your family, so they'll always
look forward to coming home.

261.
Ask Her…

if she'd help you to ask yourself,
if attitudes were contagious, would
yours be worth catching?

262.
Ask Her...

to remind you that she wants nothing more than the salvation of your soul.

263.
Ask Her...

to remind you that each time you study scripture is like a personal training session with Christ, building you into a mighty warrior for Him.

264.
Ask Her...

to encourage you to go out of your way to help make *someone else's* dream come true.

265.
Ask Her...

to give you the spiritual fortitude to not only endure your own suffering, but to pray that it will be used to redeem others.

266.
Ask Her...

if she'd help you learn to affirm, honor, and celebrate the small things.

267.
Ask Her...

to remind you that the more simplicity you bring into your life, the more liberated you will feel.

268.
Ask Her...

to remind you that you're crowned with steadfast love and tender mercy through Christ. So, straighten your crown, child, and don't let anyone take it from you.

269.
Ask Her...

to remind you that by expressing gratitude aloud, you amplify it.

270.

Ask Her...

to open your eyes so you can clearly see the difference between the things you really *want* and the things you really *need*.

271.

Ask Her...

to remind you that God's word does not obscure. It will not keep you guessing. Rather, it illuminates your path. It shows you the truth.

272.

Ask Her...

if she'd remind you that it is often your pursuit to control things tomorrow that contributes to your worry today.

273.

Ask Her...

to not let you be deceived into thinking that you should bear your suffering alone. It is in your willingness to be transparent *while* you're wrestling with it that you become a courageous witness to the people around you.

274.

Ask Her...

to help you begin transforming your life from worried and fearful to unshakable and fearless.

275.

Ask Her...

to remind you that it is through the actions by which you treat your enemies that you show the world the most compelling example of the character of God.

276.
Ask Her...

to reassure you that you are *not* defined by what you're most ashamed of. Don't give your past the power to define your future.

277.
Ask Her...

to pray with you for an outpouring of the Holy Spirit on every member of your family.

278.
Ask Her...

to help you remember that a part of being kind is being kind to yourself.

279.
Ask Her...

to help you remember if you're seeking the mercy of God, practice being merciful.

280.

Ask Her...

to remind you that the *real* authentic love for which you long for can only be found with God.

281.

Ask Her...

to help you remember that every time you make the hard choice to do what's right, you bring the world closer to God.

282.
Ask Her...

to remind you that everything changes or passes away...except God.

283.
Ask Her...

when you're scared, if she'd wrap you tightly in the warmth and protection of her mantle.

284.

Ask Her...

to not only teach you about holiness, but help you grow in it a little each day.

285.

Ask Her...

if God is encouraging a change in your life, to infuse you with the strength and courage you'll need to embark on the journey.

286.

Ask Her...

for her Immaculate Heart
to triumph in our sinful world.

287.

Ask Her...

to keep reminding you of the
great graces that come when you're
able to pray for God's best for the
people who antagonize you the most.

288.
Ask Her...

to remind you when you put God first in your family, you set a firm foundation for everything else.

289.
Ask Her...

to remind you that God promises to be with you, guide you, and direct your steps when you're feeling hesitant about a decision.

290.
Ask Her...

to carry you further and further into
the marvelous love of the Father.

291.
Ask Her...

to pray for God to unleash
His almighty power within you when
you feel weak and discouraged.

292.
Ask Her...

to help take away every ounce of
hatred and jealousy within you.

293.
Ask Her...

to guide you into a new time
of grace that will embolden a more
vulnerable and braver version of you.

294.
Ask Her...

if today she would help you remember to let go and let God.

295.
Ask Her...

to remind you that when you live a Christ-centered life, you are collaborating with God in the work of salvation.

296.

Ask Her...

to reaffirm how God's most important stories aren't told from a podium to thousands of people, but in the everyday encounters people have with God.

297.

Ask Her...

to remind you that her fervent prayer is for you to experience the abundant life God gives when you submit yourself completely to Him.

298.

Ask Her...

to help you see that spiritual knowledge is a uniquely personal journey that begins at the feet of Jesus.

299.

Ask Her...

to help draw out of you all the goodness God has poured into you.

300.

Ask Her...

to help you understand that it isn't about you and your sins — it's about Jesus and His mercy.

301.

Ask Her...

to help you stand firm, persevering in faith, and believing that God will come through for you, ALWAYS!

302.

Ask Her...

to keep reminding you what the angel said: "Do not be afraid. God is with you."

303.

Ask Her...

to tenderly reveal how the love of the Father is immeasurably bigger than your imperfections...and His mercies are new *every single morning!*

304.
Ask Her...

if she would give you a divine patience to deal with things that may exasperate and agitate you.

305.
Ask Her...

to help you pray for the homebound and isolated, that God would be their supernatural source of comfort when they feel most lonely.

306.

Ask Her...

to help you remember when
your heart is broken, she will always
be there to help you pick up the
pieces and begin again.

307.

Ask Her...

to reaffirm that rejections and setbacks
will often lead you down the path you
were meant to take. TRUST!

308.

Ask Her...

to remind you that prayer is but a meeting of the hearts: yours and her Son's.

309.

Ask Her...

if she would be a constant reminder that you were created for a unique purpose, and that the gifts God's given you need to be shared with this world.

310.

Ask Her...

to remind you to be generous
with your attention.

311.

Ask Her...

to infuse you with all the courage
and humility it takes to make amends
with anyone you've harmed.

312.

Ask Her...

to remind you that you can find God in *everything*, even in the most minuscule, infinitesimal things.

313.

Ask Her...

to remind you that she knows from experience just how life-changing the word "Yes" is.

314.

Ask Her...

to help you renounce all the worldly things you're attached to that might be hindering you from attaining the spiritual life you long for.

315.

Ask Her...

to reassure you that you will have God's very best, because that's what He promised.

316.

Ask Her...

if you're wrestling with doubt, seek with a sincere heart, and she will accompany you on the journey toward truth.

317.

Ask Her...

to remind you that more than anything, she wants to see you overflowing with God's love. So much so, it flows out from you and over those around you.

318.

Ask Her...

to remind you how you'll ALWAYS find the tenderness of a mother's heart when you approach her in prayer.

319.

Ask Her...

to remind you, if you want to hear the voice of God, first find a quiet place, then surrender yourself to the Holy Spirit and listen.

320.

Ask Her...

if she would help you learn that
it's only by acknowledging your faults
and weaknesses that you can work to
change them into virtues and strengths.

321.

Ask Her...

to reaffirm that you don't have to
justify your devotion to her — when you
honor her, you honor her Son.

322.

Ask Her...

to remind you, before your feet touch the floor each morning, to put on the full Armor of God.

323.

Ask Her...

to remind you that you are a victor, not a victim.

324.
Ask Her...

to help you remember that when she and God are for you, no one can be against you.

325.
Ask Her...

to pray that God would answer the cries of couples desperate to be parents and who are having difficulty conceiving.

326.
Ask Her...

to remind you that life is about progress, not perfection.

327.
Ask Her...

to remind you that *what you value* is reflected in *how you live*.

328.

Ask Her...

to help you recognize that it is only when *your* heart is at peace can you then spread peace in the world.

329.

Ask Her...

to impede any anger, bitterness, or resentment threatening to take up permanent residence in your heart.

330.

Ask Her...

to be a constant reminder that, while you can't control people or circumstances in life, you *can* control your attitude toward them.

331.

Ask Her...

to let the power of God's love break through all those lies telling you you're not good enough, strong enough, or that you can't get through it.

332.

Ask Her...

to reveal how sharing difficult or embarrassing circumstances can often be the answered prayer of those who thought they were alone.

333.

Ask Her...

to remind you that hopelessness is the inability to see the unlimited potential of God.

334.
Ask Her...

to help you to see the tremendous anointing that occurs when you willingly decrease, so God can increase.

335.
Ask Her...

to teach you how to invoke the Holy Spirit to help you determine what needs to be said and what needs to be left unsaid.

336.

Ask Her...

to help you make God your refuge, your safe place, your retreat, the place you can go when you are afraid.

337.

Ask Her...

to remember that the way to restore unity in humanity is learning to respect each other's differences and working to find common ground.

338.

Ask Her...

to water and nurture the seeds God planted in you so they will produce a fruitful harvest for His Kingdom.

339.

Ask Her...

to help you be the one to have the courage to step up when someone is being bullied or excluded.

340.

Ask Her...

to remind you that life on this earth is merely a pilgrimage toward home.

341.

Ask Her...

to help you remember that the fruit of peace is love and the fruit of love is forgiveness.

342.
Ask Her...

to remind you, if you only do things with your own strength, you will never know the power of God.

343.
Ask Her...

to help you remain steadfast and faithful in your journey even when it's difficult.

344.

Ask Her...

to help you remember that Christ is your spiritual teacher and advocate. Don't ever hesitate to ask questions.

345.

Ask Her...

to remind you, when you commit to love, you fulfill the very meaning of your existence.

346.

Ask Her...

to help you become a guiding influence who embodies goodness and selflessness, who is tenderhearted and considerate.

347.

Ask Her...

to remind you that God does not want fear to dictate your life, but Satan does.

348.

Ask Her...

to remind you how, every time she looks at you, she sees the Divine Architect building something extraordinary.

349.

Ask Her...

to help you remember not to let today cloud who you will be tomorrow.

350.

Ask Her...

to help you understand how unfair it is to presume to know what is best for another person.

351.

Ask Her...

to help you exceed someone's expectations today.

352.

Ask Her...

to help you be still when
you're tangled up in turmoil.
She is slowly and methodically
working to loosen the knots.

353.

Ask Her...

to remind you that God really
needs you to meet people
where they are, not where you
think they should be.

354.

Ask Her...

to help you remember what a sacred gift it is to be entrusted with someone else's heart, to humbly care for their feelings, and to actively desire their happiness.

355.

Ask Her...

to remind you when you need more hope, more healing, more patience, or more authentic joy, she's got a personal connection with the One who can help.

356.

Ask Her...

to remind you that every day you have an opportunity to influence someone else's life forever, to make a difference...an eternal difference.

357.

Ask Her...

to remind you that *speaking the truth* is never bad, but it's *how you speak the truth* that makes all the difference.

358.

Ask Her...

to remind you that you don't have
to have money to have a generous heart.
The richness of the gift comes from
the motive, not the checkbook.

359.

Ask Her...

to remind you that love speaks
fluently in every language.

360.

Ask Her...

to help you remember that getting where you want to go in life is a process. It's within the process that life unfolds. Let yourself be captivated by the process.

361.

Ask Her...

to help you remember that God is the restorer of broken things.

362.

Ask Her...

to remind you of how reconciliation reconnects what sin disconnects.

363.

Ask Her...

to remind you that Jesus waits for you. He waits to take your burdens, to lighten your load, and to love you exactly as you are.

364.

Ask Her...

to remind you that God chose YOU before He ever created the Heavens and the earth! Before He formed you in the womb, He knew you. His hands knitted and fashioned you together and made you. You are completely accepted, unconditionally loved, and totally forgiven. You are known and seen. He delights and rejoices over you with joy. He surrounds you, protects you, and guards your heart. He will never leave you nor turn away from you. Your identity in Christ is secure. Claim it and rest in it!

365.

Ask Her...

to remind you that you'll never comprehend the magnitude in which she loves you, it's that magnanimous.

JANE TRUFANT HARVEY is the author of the popular gift book series *Ask Him for Encouragement, Ask Him for Hope, Thank Him, Saints Alive,* and *Ask Him For Courage With Cancer*.

Jane is an avid reader and enthusiastic golfer and an indefatigable community volunteer. She cherishes time with her family. She and her husband Bobby have been married for 44 years and are the proud parents of four children Elizabeth, Lauren, Bobby, III and Taylor. They have five precious grandchildren, Cade Nicolas, Austin Joseph, Emily Joyce, Olivia Jane, and Robert Gerard, IV. You can email Jane at info@askhimbooks.com.